SPORTS' WILDEST UPSETS

# PRO HOCKEY UPSETS

WILL GRAVES

Lerner Publications ◆ Minneapolis

Lerner Publications Company
An imprint of Lerner Publishing Group, Inc.
241 First Avenue North
Minneapolis, MN 55401 USA

For reading levels and more information, look up this title at www.lernerbooks.com.

Main body text set in Aptifer Sans LT Pro.
Typeface provided by Linotype AG.

**Library of Congress Cataloging-in-Publication Data**

Names: Graves, Will, author.
Title: Pro hockey upsets / by Will Graves.
Description: Minneapolis : Lerner Publications, [2020] | Series: Sports' wildest upsets
    (Lerner Spots) | Includes bibliographical references and index. | Audience: Age 7–11. |
    Audience: K to Grade 3.
Identifiers: LCCN 2019017251 (print) | LCCN 2019022343 (ebook) | ISBN 9781541577114
    (lb : alk. paper) | ISBN 9781541589681 (pb : alk. paper)
Subjects: LCSH: Hockey—Juvenile literature. | Sports upsets—Juvenile literature.
Classification: LCC GV847.25 .G73 2020  (print) | LCC GV847.25  (ebook) | DDC 796.962—
    dc23

LC record available at https://lccn.loc.gov/2019017251

Manufactured in the United States of America
1 – CG – 12/31/19

# CONTENTS

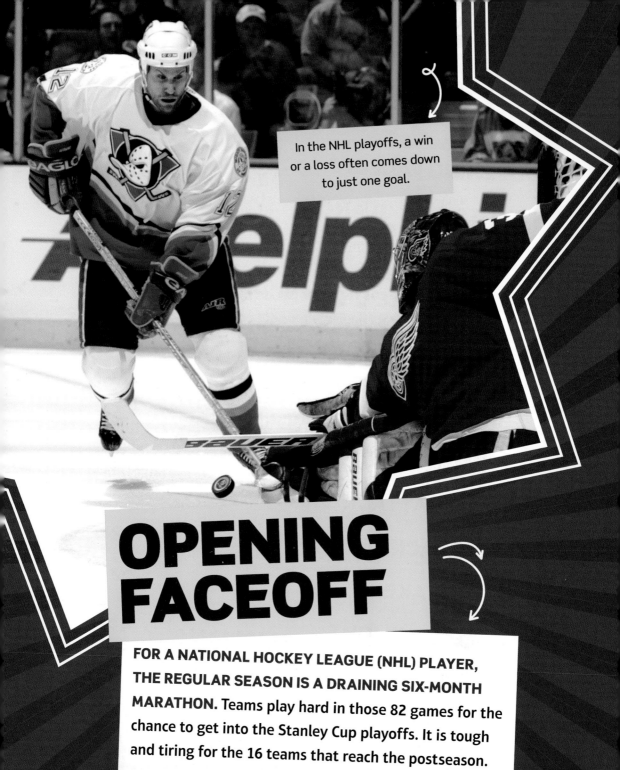

In the NHL playoffs, a win or a loss often comes down to just one goal.

# OPENING FACEOFF

**FOR A NATIONAL HOCKEY LEAGUE (NHL) PLAYER, THE REGULAR SEASON IS A DRAINING SIX-MONTH MARATHON.** Teams play hard in those 82 games for the chance to get into the Stanley Cup playoffs. It is tough and tiring for the 16 teams that reach the postseason.

During the playoffs, every team gets an opportunity to start over. It doesn't matter if the team had a great season or an average one. Any team in the playoffs has a shot at the Stanley Cup.

Games are fast and full of action. And any player can have a huge impact. A center can speed down the ice on a breakaway and shoot a slap shot into the goal to take the lead. Similarly, one key save by a goalie can determine who brings home the Stanley Cup. The pace of the game means that things can change in an instant.

## FACTS AT A GLANCE

- With the legendary Wayne Gretzky leading the way, the 1982 Edmonton Oilers were expected to beat the Los Angeles Kings for the Stanley Cup. But the Kings surprised everyone when they beat the Oilers in five games during the opening round of the playoffs.

- Montreal Canadiens goalie Jaroslav Halak dominated in the first round of the 2010 Stanley Cup playoffs against the Washington Capitals. In the last three games of the series, he stopped 131 out of 134 shots, leading Montreal to the win.

- The Vegas Golden Knights were added to the NHL as an **expansion team** in 2017. Expected to be one of the worst teams in the league, the Knights went against all odds to win. They become the first expansion team to win three playoff series and reach the Stanley Cup Final in its first year.

# GOLDEN BOYS

LITTLE WAS EXPECTED OF THE NHL'S NEWEST TEAM, THE VEGAS GOLDEN KNIGHTS, IN 2017–2018. Expansion teams tend to be bad, since they are usually made up of players other teams didn't want. The Golden Knights began the season with a 500-to-1 odds to win the Stanley Cup.

One of the Vegas Golden Knights' regular season wins in 2017 was against the Dallas Stars.

William Karlsson skates down the ice for the Golden Knights in Game 3 against the San Jose Sharks.

But then Vegas won its first game of the year. The team won its second and third-ever games too. The wins kept piling up over the next six months. The Knights posted a record of 51–24–7. They won the Pacific Division.

The Knights' wild ride kept going in the playoffs. They swept the Los Angeles Kings in the first round. They took out the San Jose Sharks in the second. Then they were up against the second-**seeded** Winnipeg Jets in the Western Conference finals.

The Winnipeg Jets had the second-best record in the NHL in the 2017–2018 season.

The Jets breezed through Game 1 with a 4–2 win. Then the Knights beat the Jets the next three games. The Knights could move on to the Stanley Cup Final if they won Game 5.

Five minutes into the first period, Alex Tuch of the Knights scored off a turnover. Winnipeg came back to tie the game. Then Vegas' Luca Sbisa shot from the point and teammate Ryan Reaves tipped it into the goal in the second period.

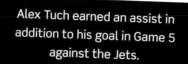

Alex Tuch earned an assist in addition to his goal in Game 5 against the Jets.

The Knights held the lead for the rest of the game. They became the first expansion team to win three playoff series and reach the Stanley Cup Final in its first year.

The Knights didn't get the storybook ending they were hoping for. They fell to the Washington Capitals in the Stanley Cup Final. But Vegas' amazing run made NHL history.

FINAL SERIES SCORE

GOLDEN KNIGHTS | JETS
4 | 1

Wayne Gretzky is one of the most famous hockey players of all time.

# THE MIRACLE ON MANCHESTER

**THE 1981–1982 EDMONTON OILERS WERE LED BY SUPERSTAR WAYNE GRETZKY.** They were considered a heavy **favorite** against the Los Angeles Kings during the Stanley Cup playoffs.

Then Edmonton fell apart. The Kings won Game 1. The Oilers scraped by in Game 2 with a 3–2 win. On April 10, 1982, with a 5–0 lead in the third period, the Oilers seemed sure to win Game 3.

The Los Angeles Kings' win against the Edmonton Oilers is called the "Miracle on Manchester" because the arena the game took place in was on Manchester Boulevard.

Then the Kings scored five times during the final 20 minutes to force **overtime**. The LA crowd went wild. Two and a half minutes into overtime, Los Angeles **rookie** Daryl Evans hit a slap shot deep into the back left corner of the net.

The victory gave the Kings a 2–1 lead in the best-of-five series. Though Edmonton took Game 4, Los Angeles was able to win the series in the deciding Game 5.

The 1982 Oilers are considered one of the best teams in NHL history to come up short of a championship.

# THE KINGS OUTSCORED

Gretzky is one of the all-time greats in hockey, and he played well during the playoff series. He had five goals and seven assists. But Los Angeles still outscored Edmonton 27–23 to advance.

**FINAL SERIES SCORE**

| KINGS | OILERS |
|-------|--------|
| 3 | 2 |

# AN UPSET WITH A CAPITAL "U"

THE WASHINGTON CAPITALS WERE ON TOP OF THE WORLD COMING INTO THE 2010 STANLEY CUP PLAYOFFS. They had the most wins and had scored the most goals in the NHL. And they were the top-seeded team in the Eastern Conference. They were ready to plow through the Montreal Canadiens in the first round.

The Montreal Canadiens went into the 2010 playoffs with a 39-33-10 record. The Washington Capitals' record was 54-15-13.

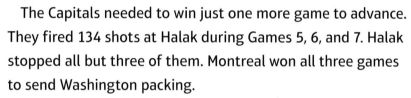

Capitals' star Alex Ovechkin (*right*) appeared to be devastated after Jaroslav Halak helped the Canadiens win Game 7.

Washington raced to a quick 3–1 lead in the series. But then Jaroslav Halak of the Canadiens became, for a few days anyway, the best goalie on the planet.

The Capitals needed to win just one more game to advance. They fired 134 shots at Halak during Games 5, 6, and 7. Halak stopped all but three of them. Montreal won all three games to send Washington packing.

"Some people didn't give us a chance to even win one game," Halak said. "They were wrong. This team showed a lot of character." And they took down a heavy favorite in the process.

FINAL SERIES SCORE

CANADIENS | CAPITALS

4 | 3

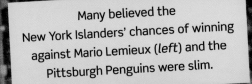

Many believed the New York Islanders' chances of winning against Mario Lemieux (*left*) and the Pittsburgh Penguins were slim.

# ISLANDERS SILENCE SUPER MARIO

**THE 1993 PITTSBURGH PENGUINS WERE THE TWO-TIME DEFENDING STANLEY CUP CHAMPIONS.** Powered by superstar center Mario Lemieux, nicknamed "Super Mario," the Penguins rolled past the New Jersey Devils in the opening round of the Stanley Cup playoffs. The second round of playoffs against the New York Islanders was expected to be more of the same.

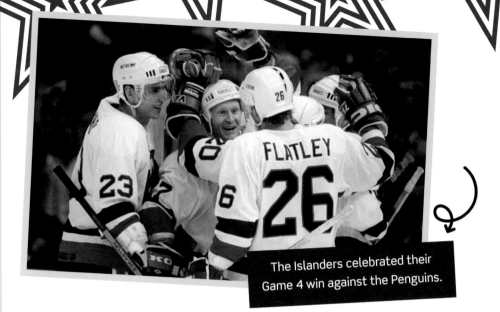

The Islanders celebrated their Game 4 win against the Penguins.

However, the **underdog** Islanders shot the puck well and proved they could play with the champions. New York pushed the series to Game 7. There, Pittsburgh ruled the ice, shooting twice as often as New York. But New York led 3–1 with four minutes remaining. Then Pittsburgh scored twice to force overtime.

Instead of crumbling, the Islanders shined. Five minutes into the extra period, New York's Ray Ferraro and David Volek made a break down the ice. Ferraro passed to Volek, who took the shot. The puck whizzed past goaltender Tom Barrasso. The goal ended Pittsburgh's bid to win the Stanley Cup three years in a row.

## WINNING STREAK

Pittsburgh's 17-game winning streak to finish off the regular season is the longest in NHL history. The Islanders' longest winning streak in 1992–1993 was just five games.

FINAL SERIES SCORE

| ISLANDERS | PENGUINS |
|---|---|
| 4 | 3 |

# PANTHERS' UNLIKELY RUN

**THE FLORIDA PANTHERS EARNED A TRIP TO THE 1996 PLAYOFFS.** It was only their third year in the NHL. The Panthers then beat the Boston Bruins and the Philadelphia Flyers on their way to the Eastern Conference finals.

The Florida Panthers traded wins with the Pittsburgh Penguins during the competitive 1996 Eastern Conference finals.

Florida was matched up against Mario Lemieux and the mighty Pittsburgh Penguins. A trip to the Stanley Cup Final was on the line.

Thanks in large part to goalie John Vanbiesbrouck, the Panthers were able to hold their own against the Penguins. The series went to Game 7. Vanbiesbrouck stopped 39 shots in that game alone. The Panthers also brought a good offense. Florida's Tom Fitzgerald took a shot in the third period from just inside the blue line. The puck bounced off the stick of a Penguins player and went into the net. Fitzgerald's incredible goal clinched the win for the Panthers and earned the franchise an unlikely spot in the Stanley Cup Final.

The Panthers couldn't contain their excitement after their 3–1 Game 7 win.

## ONLY TIME IN HISTORY

The Panthers' 1996 postseason run remains the only time in the team's history that Florida has won a playoff series. They lost in the first round in each of their four other playoff appearances through 2019.

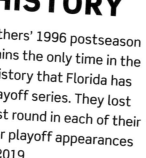

FINAL SERIES SCORE

PANTHERS | PENGUINS
4 | 3

The 1994 San Jose Sharks had a 33–35–16 regular season record.

# SHARK ATTACK

**THE SAN JOSE SHARKS SHOWED LITTLE BITE WHEN THEY ENTERED THE NHL AS AN EXPANSION TEAM IN 1991.** They finished with the fewest points in the NHL in each of their first two seasons. But by playing strong defense, San Jose made the playoffs in the 1993–1994 season. They were the eighth seed in the Western Conference.

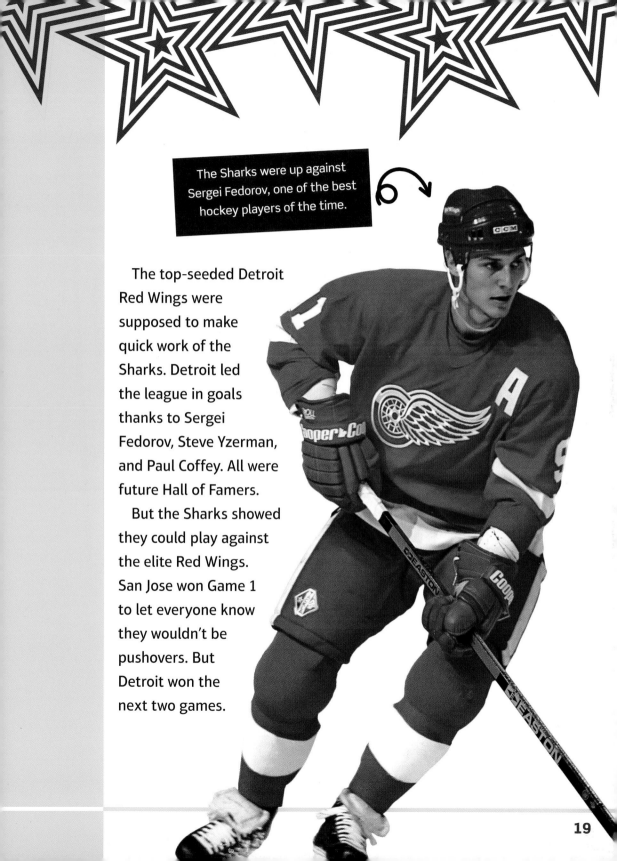

The Sharks were up against Sergei Fedorov, one of the best hockey players of the time.

The top-seeded Detroit Red Wings were supposed to make quick work of the Sharks. Detroit led the league in goals thanks to Sergei Fedorov, Steve Yzerman, and Paul Coffey. All were future Hall of Famers.

But the Sharks showed they could play against the elite Red Wings. San Jose won Game 1 to let everyone know they wouldn't be pushovers. But Detroit won the next two games.

Ulf Dahlen (22) scored the Sharks' only goal in Game 6.

The Red Wings were in the lead for most of Game 4, but the Sharks came back. San Jose's Igor Larionov scored eight minutes into the second period. Then Ulf Dahlen scored on a **power play** for the Sharks. Another goal in the third period won it for San Jose. San Jose also won Game 5. Then Detroit destroyed the Sharks 7–1 in Game 6 to force a winner-take-all Game 7.

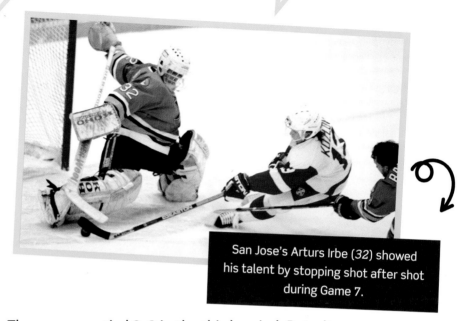

San Jose's Arturs Irbe (*32*) showed his talent by stopping shot after shot during Game 7.

The game was tied 2–2 in the third period. Detroit goaltender Chris Osgood tried to clear the puck up the boards. Sharks forward Jamie Baker pounced on the puck and fired a slap shot. It zipped to the back of the net before Osgood could get back in position. San Jose goaltender Arturs Irbe protected the lead. The Sharks held on for a 3–2 victory. They became the first team since the 1975 New York Islanders to win a series in their first-ever playoffs.

FINAL SERIES SCORE

SHARKS **4** | RED WINGS **3**

# BLUE JACKETS SHOCK ALL

**THE TAMPA BAY LIGHTNING MADE HEADLINES IN 2018-2019.** The Lightning had won 62 games. They tied the NHL record for most regular season games won. There was no reason to expect them to stop winning in the playoffs.

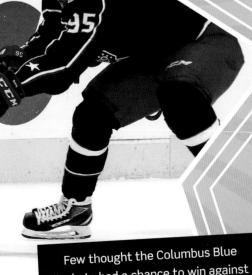

Few thought the Columbus Blue Jackets had a chance to win against the Tampa Bay Lightning.

But their first-round opponents, the Columbus Blue Jackets, weren't as easy to beat as the Lightning thought. Although the team had a mediocre season, Columbus won the first three games.

Columbus started out strong again in Game 4. By the end of the second period, the Blue Jackets had a 4–3 lead. Then Tampa Bay chose to pull its goalie. This allowed the Lightning to have an extra skater on the ice. It also allowed the Blue Jackets to come in and score more goals on an empty net.

Artemi Panarin and Alexandre Texier scored empty net goals for Columbus with less than two minutes remaining. Then Matt Duchene added another empty net goal, clinching a 7–3 win for the Blue Jackets. Columbus' **sweep** was one of the most shocking upsets in NHL history.

Columbus' Matt Duchene scored in three of the four games against Tampa Bay.

FINAL SERIES SCORE

BLUE JACKETS | LIGHTNING
4 | 0

The San Jose Sharks scored 43 more goals than the Los Angeles Kings during the 2013–2014 season.

# KING MAKERS

**BEING DOWN 3-0 IN THE FIRST ROUND OF THE PLAYOFFS IS ENOUGH TO MAKE MOST TEAMS WANT TO PACK IT IN.** The 2013–2014 Los Angeles Kings, however, were not like most teams. They believed they could beat the San Jose Sharks if they pulled together.

Tanner Pearson scored for the Kings with less than a minute left in Game 7.

"We're going to have to come back in a couple days and throw everything at them," Los Angeles star Anze Kopitar said after the Kings lost Game 3 in overtime.

And they did. The Kings turned up their defense and won by three goals in Games 4, 5, and 6. The Kings surprised just about everyone by making it to Game 7. The Kings continued to play strong defense. Los Angeles goaltender Jonathan Quick proved himself by stopping 39 shots in Game 7. And offensive players like Kopitar and Tanner Pearson helped the Kings sink the Sharks 5–1.

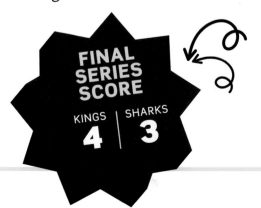

FINAL SERIES SCORE

KINGS | SHARKS
4 | 3

# PHILLY'S FLIGHT

**THE 2009-2010 PHILADELPHIA FLYERS DIDN'T EARN A PLAYOFF SPOT UNTIL THE FINAL GAME OF THE REGULAR SEASON.** They beat the New York Rangers 2–1 in an overtime shootout to take the last postseason spot.

The Philadelphia Flyers beat the New Jersey Devils 4-1 in the first round of the 2010 playoffs.

Simon Gagné scored four goals for the Flyers in the seven games against the Boston Bruins.

The Flyers breezed past the New Jersey Devils in the first round but fell behind 3–0 against the Boston Bruins in the Eastern Conference semifinals.

Simon Gagné kept the season alive with an overtime goal in Game 4 to defeat the Bruins 5–4. It was the spark the Flyers needed. Two more wins followed, pushing the series to Game 7.

The Bruins appeared to be in good shape when they scored three times in the first 14 minutes. But the Flyers ripped off the next four goals. Gagné's power play goal in the middle of the third period capped an unlikely win.

## DOWN THREE TO WIN

Philadelphia's rally marked just the third time a team had come back from a three-game deficit in the playoffs to win. The 1975 New York Islanders did it to the Penguins. And the Toronto Maple Leafs upset the Red Wings in 1942.

### FINAL SERIES SCORE

| FLYERS | BRUINS |
| --- | --- |
| 4 | 3 |

# OVERTIME

**THE NHL BEGAN IN 1917, AND THE MODERN ERA STARTED IN 1942 WITH SIX TEAMS.** The league added several expansion teams over the years. By 2019, there were 31 teams in the league, with a 32nd set to join in 2021.

NHL playoff games are often unpredictable.

Every NHL team's goal is to hold up the Stanley Cup at the end of the season.

More teams means many more chances for upsets. The NHL playoffs have some of the most unpredictable games of any sport. Beating another team four times takes hard work, determination, and faith in yourself and your teammates, even if it looks like all is lost. If a team has time left, they have a chance to win.

Playoff games have led to some of the greatest moments in the history of the sport. While there can only be one winner of the Stanley Cup, all playoff teams have a chance to make NHL history.

# SOURCE NOTES

13  *CBC.CA*, "Canadiens Upset Capitals in Game 7 Stunner," 28 May 2019, https://www.cbc.ca/sports/hockey/nhl/canadiens-upset-capitals-in-game-7-stunner-1.887285.

25  *USA Today*, "Sharks Beat Kings 4–3 in OT, Take 3–0 Series Lead," 28 May 2019, https://www.usatoday.com/story/sports/nhl/2014/04/23/sharks-beat-kings-4-3-in-ot-take-3-0-series-lead/8040403.

# GLOSSARY

**expansion team:** a team that is added to an established league

**favorite:** expected to win

**overtime:** an extra period of play when the score is tied after regulation

**power play:** when one team has more players than their opponent on the ice because of a penalty

**rookie:** a first-year player

**seeded:** ranked compared to the rest of the teams in a tournament

**sweep:** to win a series of games without any losses

**underdog:** a team that is expected to lose against an opponent

# FURTHER INFORMATION

ESPN: NHL
http://www.espn.com/nhl

Herman, Gail. *What Is the Stanley Cup?*
New York: Penguin Workshop, 2019.

NHL.com
www.nhl.com

Page, Sam. *Hockey: Then to WOW.* New York: Time Inc. Books, 2017.

Sports Illustrated Kids: Hockey
https://www.sikids.com/hockey

Zweig, Eric. *Hockey Hall of Fame Heroes: Scorers, Goalies and Defensemen.* Richmond Hill, Ontario: Firefly Books, 2016.

# INDEX

# PHOTO ACKNOWLEDGMENTS

The images in this book are used with the permission of: © Jeff Gross/NHLI/Getty Images Sport/Getty Images, p. 4; © Tom Pennington/Getty Images Sport/Getty Images, p. 6; © Ezra Shaw/Getty Images Sport/Getty Images, p. 7; © Darcy Finley/NHLI/National Hockey League/Getty Images, pp. 8, 9; © Reed Saxon/AP Images, p. 10; © Doug Pizac/AP Images, p. 11; © Mitchell Layton/NHLI/National Hockey League/Getty Images, p. 12; © Bruce Bennett/Getty Images Sport/Getty Images, pp. 13, 26; © Paul Hurschmann/AP Images, p. 14; © Ron Frehm/AP Images, p. 15; © Marta Lavandier/AP Images, p. 16; © Gene J. Puskar/AP Images, p. 17; © Denis Brodeur/NHLI/National Hockey League/Getty Images, p. 18; © Graig Abel/Getty Images Sport/Getty Images, p. 19; © Lennox McLendon/AP Images, pp. 20, 21; © Kirk Irwin/Getty Images Sport/Getty Images, p. 22; © Jamie Sabau/NHLI/National Hockey League/Getty Images, p. 23; © Thearon W. Henderson/Getty Images Sport/Getty Images, p. 24; © Chris Williams/Icon Sportswire/Getty Images, p. 25; © Len Redkoles/NHLI/National Hockey League/Getty Images, p. 27; © Brian Bahr/NHLI/Getty Images Sport/Getty Images, p. 28; © Jim McIsaac/Getty Images Sport/Getty Images, p. 29.

Front Cover: © B Bennett/Bruce Bennett/Getty Images, top left; © Len Redkoles/NHLI/National Hockey League/Getty Images, top right; © Jonathan Kozub/NHLI/National Hockey League/Getty Images, bottom.